SLAVIC PAGAN ROOTS: DECODING THE PRIMARY CHRONICLE

BY.

PERUN MOUNTAIN

First published by Perun Mountain
www.PerunMountain.com
Copyright © 2024 by Perun Mountain

All rights reserved. No part of this publication may be reproduced, stored, or transmitted in any form or by any means, electronic, mechanical, photocopying, recording, scanning, or otherwise, without written permission from the publisher. It is illegal to copy this book, post it to a website, or distribute it by any other means without permission.

Perun Mountain asserts the moral and legal right to be identified as the author of this work.

First edition
ISBN: 9798324280451

Published by

Perun Mountain
PO Box 110
Gorham, New Hampshire, 03581
United States of America.

DEDICATION

To the ancestral voices echoing through the ages, whispering ancient wisdom into the modern mind. To the seekers who unearth and share knowledge long obscured and suppressed. This book is a sacred offering.

To the chroniclers of "The Primary Chronicle," whose efforts to document their present have unwittingly allowed us a window into a world they sought to transform and erase.

May this exploration into the depths of Slavic paganism illuminate the ancient bonds between earth, sky, and the human heart, celebrating a legacy that transcends the intent of its original recorders and continues to inspire those who walk the earth today

TABLE OF CONTENTS

INTRODUCTION 1

THE PRIMARY CHRONICLE 7

SLAVIC PAGANISM 14

TRIBAL CUSTOMS IN SLAVIC SOCIETIES C/13-14 22

    COLUMN. 13–14 - THE PRIMARY CHRONICLE 25

THE FIRST TREATY: PAGAN DIPLOMACY C/32 27

    COLUMN. 32 - THE PRIMARY CHRONICLE 29

THE SECOND TREATY: SWEARING BY THE SWORD C/33 30

    COLUMN. 33 - THE PRIMARY CHRONICLE 32

THE LEGEND OF PRINCE OLEG: FATE AND PROPHECY. C/38–39 33

    COLUMN. 38-39 - THE PRIMARY CHRONICLE 35

THE THIRD TREATY: PERUN'S HILL C47-48, 53 AND 54 37

    COLUMN. 47-48 & 53-54 - THE PRIMARY CHRONICLE 39

RITUALS OF REVENGE AND FUNERARY TRADITIONS- C/55-57 42

    COLUMN. 55-57 - THE PRIMARY CHRONICLE 44

THE PAGAN OATHS OF SVJATOSLAV'S TREATY C/73 47

    COLUMN. 73 - THE PRIMARY CHRONICLE 49

THE SLAVIC DEITIES, SACRIFICES, AND IDOLS HILL. C/79 50

COLUMN. 79 - THE PRIMARY CHRONICLE 52

THE CLASH OF FAITHS: PAGAN RESISTANCE C/82–83 54

COLUMN. 82-83 - THE PRIMARY CHRONICLE 56

VLADIMIR'S CONVERSION: THE FALL OF THE IDOLS C/116-117 59

COLUMN. 116-117 - THE PRIMARY CHRONICLE 62

VLADIMIR'S FINAL JOURNEY: BURIAL AND TRADITION C/140 63

COLUMN. 140 - THE PRIMARY CHRONICLE 65

SORCERERS' UPRISING AND RELIGIOUS TENSIONS, C/147-148 66

COLUMN. 147-148- THE PRIMARY CHRONICLE 68

VSESLAV BIRTH PHENOMENA, C/155 69

COLUMN. 155 - THE PRIMARY CHRONICLE 71

THE NOMADIC INVASION AND THE RUSALIAS, C/170 72

COLUMN. 170- THE PRIMARY CHRONICLE 74

SORCERY IN 1071 KIEVAN RUS, C/174–175 75

COLUMN. 174-175 - THE PRIMARY CHRONICLE 77

SORCERY, REBELLION, AND RELIGIOUS SYNCRETISM, C/175–178 78

COLUMN. 175-178 - THE PRIMARY CHRONICLE 80

CROSS-CULTURAL ENCOUNTERS IN MAGIC, C/179 84

COLUMN. 179 - THE PRIMARY CHRONICLE 86

DEAD AMONG THE LIVING C/208 87

COLUMN. 208 - THE PRIMARY CHRONICLE 89

SUPERNATURAL PHENOMENA & THE INFERNAL HUNT, C./214–215 90

COLUMN. 214-215 - THE PRIMARY CHRONICLE 92

SVAROG AND DAZHBOG: BRIDGING SLAVIC DEITIES C./278–279 93

COLUMN. 278-279 - THE PRIMARY CHRONICLE 95

CONCLUSION 97

ABOUT THE AUTHORS 100

INTRODUCTION

A chronicle of unparalleled depth and complexity emerged in the shadow of medieval Kievan Rus' amidst the convergence of rivers and the expanse of dense forests that whispered the ancient secrets of the Slavic people. The manuscript, known as The Primary Chronicle or Повѣстъ временьныхъ лѣтъ in Old East Slavonic, stands as a monumental beacon in the murky waters of Slavic history, guiding us through the interplay of darkness and light that characterized the era's spiritual battleground. Here, in this meticulously compiled narrative, we witness the eternal dance between the ancient pagan traditions, deeply rooted in the Slavic spirit, and the relentless advance of a foreign faith known as Christianity. This force sought to redefine the very essence of divinity and morals in the vast and complex lands of the Slavs.

Created by monastic scribes at the dawn of the 12th century, this chronicle offers an unparalleled window into Slavic native customs, mythologies, and spiritual practices that flourished across modern Central and Eastern Europe. Despite the chroniclers' Christian biases, which cast a shadow of skepticism over some ancient rites, their writings inadvertently serve as a vessel for preserving a wealth of pagan lore.

In the seclusion of their monasteries, the Chronicle scribes did not write this text merely as an act of historical record but to build a bridge to an unknown world. This world of the ancient Slavs was vibrant with myths, where every grove and river was ensouled, and the skies above were a battleground for divine beings of immense power. Yet, the chroniclers, viewed through the lens of their Christian faith, described these traditions with a mix of fascination and criticism.

As we read into the sections of the Primary Chronicle, we are invited into the realm of the Slavic pantheon, a complex hierarchy of gods and goddesses that governed every facet of human existence. At the pinnacle of this divine assembly sat Perun, the god of thunder and lightning, his mighty axe crackling with the storm's force. Perun was not just a figure of awe and reverence; he symbolized the unyielding strength of the natural world, the sudden and terrifying beauty of a thunderstorm that could, in a moment, nourish the earth or bring it to ruin.

Contrasting Perun's fiery dominion was Veles, the elusive deity of the underworld, of cattle, and of commerce, who slithered through the realms in serpentine form. Veles's domain was that of the unseen, the wealth that lies beneath the earth, and the mysteries that dwell beyond the veil of death. The conflict between Perun and Veles, a motif recurring in Slavic mythology, mirrors the eternal struggle between order and chaos, fertility and drought, life, and the shadow of death.

Yet, the pantheon was not limited to these two figures. The Chronicle whispers of Svarog, the celestial smith, forger of the sun, and his sons, Svarozhich, the fire spirits that watch over the hearths and homes. It speaks of Dazhbog, the sun god, who rides his fiery chariot across the sky, bringing light and warmth to the land. Mokosh, the earth mother, weaves her magic into the fabric of the fields, ensuring fertility and abundance. Each deity played a role in the grand cosmic drama, their stories intertwined with the lives of those who honored them.

The chroniclers recount tales of rites and festivals, of offerings made at sacred groves and by riverbanks, where the veil between the human and divine was believed to be at its thinnest. These ceremonies, marked by the moon's cycles and the seasons' turn, were not mere superstitions but the expression of a deep, symbiotic relationship with the natural world. The veneration of these gods and the observance of these rituals provided spiritual sustenance and a framework for understanding the universe and one's place.

The survival of these pagan traditions, as seen through the prism of the Primary Chronicle, is a testament to the resilience of cultural identity in the face of religious transformation. Despite the Christian overlay, the ancient practices and beliefs of the Slavic peoples endured, and their essence was preserved in the folklore and customs passed down through generations. The revival of these traditions in the modern practice of Rodnovery and Slavic Native Faith is not merely a nostalgic look back but a vibrant reclamation of a spiritual heritage that continues to inspire and guide those who seek to reconnect with the ancient ways of their ancestors. Expanding upon the journey outlined in "Slavic Pagan Roots:," we will navigate the intricate mosaic of Slavic paganism before and after the tide of Christianity swept across the Slavic lands. Our odyssey into the past seeks to uncover and breathe life into the earliest written testimonies of Slavic spirituality before the Christian conquest endeavored to reshape Eastern Europe's cultural and religious landscape. It is a pilgrimage back to a time when the Slavic identity was intertwined with the rhythms of the earth, the cycles of the sun and moon, and the reverence for nature that permeated every aspect of life.

Our quest has challenges, as our guide, The Primary Chronicle, was penned by observers outside the native faith they describe, often with a mission to discredit and erase the very traditions they document. Yet, within the lines of their biased accounts lies the potential to reconstruct a world where the Slavic Native Faith, or Slavic paganism, thrived in harmony with the natural world. The chroniclers, despite their intent to showcase the triumph of Christianity over 'pagan darkness,' inadvertently preserved a window into the soul of pre-Christian Slavic society.

The Primary Chronicle offers fleeting glimpses into the Slavic world, revealing a complex life and views that governed the forces of nature and the fate of humanity. These forces were not remote entities reigning from afar; they were integral to the community's daily life, and their gods' presence was felt in every thunderstorm, every harvest, and every turn of the season. Through rituals, offerings, and festivals, the Slavs sought to live in harmony with these divine forces, ensuring their communities' well-being and their lands' fertility.

Therefore, our examination of The Primary Chronicle must be critical. We must peer beyond the chroniclers' disdain to see the Slavs' reverence for their true faith. As we dig into The Primary Chronicle, we also encounter the darker aspects of this transition from native faith to Christianity: the destruction of idols, the desecration of sacred sites, and the persecution of those who clung to the old ways. These accounts, though painful, are integral to our understanding of this pivotal moment in Slavic history. They remind us of the resilience of Slavic paganism, which continued to influence Slavic culture and spirituality despite attempts to erase it from memory.

This is both an academic exercise and an act of reclamation and revival. By piecing together the fragments of Slavic paganism preserved in this text, we seek to offer a voice to those ancient practitioners who revered the land, the elements, and the cycles of life. In doing so, we enrich our understanding of the past and illuminate a path for those in the present drawn to explore and revive Slavic Native Faith. This journey through the pages of history is, ultimately, a journey of discovery, seeking to reconnect with a wisdom that, though buried by time and history, still holds profound relevance for our lives today.

THE PRIMARY CHRONICLE

The Primary Chronicle is an indispensable resource for studying the Kievan Rus during its pivotal formative years. While there are concerns about its objectivity and accuracy, its unparalleled contributions continue to shape our understanding of the historical narrative of this era.

Initially, the chronicle presents a somewhat disorganized narrative, but with the introduction of the first dated event (year 6360, corresponding to 852 AD), it adopts a systematic annual chronology. Each year is marked with an entry up to the chronicle's conclusion, although some years are notably absent of events. The dating system aligns with the Byzantine calendar, which calculates the Creation as occurring 5508 years before the birth of the Judeo-Christian god Christ.

The monk Nestor is traditionally credited as the chronicle's author, referred to as the Chronicle of Nestor, based on two main pieces of evidence: references to Nestor as a chronicler in the Paterik of the Kiev Monastery of the Caves and a 16th-century inscription in the Khlebnikov copy that attributes the work to "Nestor, a monk of the Feodosiy Monastery of the Caves." Nevertheless, the attribution to Nestor likely emerged in the 16th century due to conflating him with an 11th-century hagiographer of Russian saints, a view that remains prevalent in Russian scholarship.

The extent of Nestor's contribution to the chronicle, if any, remains uncertain. The work was probably a collaborative effort by various clergy members who continued to update it annually, possibly modifying and adding to the content over time. In this context, Nestor might have been one of several contributors. While some scholars attribute significant portions of the chronicle to him, others question the extent of his involvement. Another name mentioned as a compiler of The Primary Chronicle is Silvestr. Silvestr was the abbot of the Monastery of Vydubiči in Kiev in the early 12th century. He declares himself the author in an 1116 colophon preserved in copies of the Laurentian branch. While we don't know Silvestr's exact contributions - some argue he merely copied a previous version - his name provides a more solid basis than Nestor's for authorship attribution. Although the chronicle containing his signature is a second version, this version, or a copy made soon after 1116, is the oldest we can try to reconstruct.

The chroniclers drew from a long list of sources in drafting their work, including primary Greek sources, though likely read in Slavonic translations rather than original Greek. Key Byzantine chronicles used were the Chronicle of Hamartolos and its Continuation by Symeon the Logothete and the Chronicle of Malalas (via the so-called Chronographer). The Rus'-Greek treaties came from archival Constantinople records translated into Slavonic. The "Creed of Vladimir" passage derives from the Creed of Michael Synkellos, while the Revelations of Methodius of Patara sourced the 1096 entry on the Ishmaelites and northern peoples.

Written Slavic sources included several books from the Old and New Testaments, though without a complete Bible translation to Old Church Slavonic until the 15th century. So many biblical citations likely entered the chronicle indirectly via texts like the Paleja or Parimejnik collections. Here is my rewrite of the text:

The Primary Chronicle's text also incorporates oral sources, including legends from the armed retinues (družina) of warriors close to the princes. Another notable source was accounts the chroniclers heard firsthand from acquaintances who were included as such.

Several attempts have been made to reconstruct the original

form and intermediate stages that ultimately coalesced into The Primary Chronicle over time.

The Primary Chronicle was disseminated not as an isolated work but embedded within later historical compilations. Six texts, acknowledged as its direct descendants, are considered pivotal to understanding this chronicle. These texts are categorized into two main lineages: the north-eastern lineage, comprising the Laurentian, Radzivil, Trinity, and Moscow Academy chronicles, and the southern lineage, consisting of the Hypatian and Khlebnikov chronicles.

The Laurentian Chronicle, transcribed by the monk Laurentius in 1377, is the oldest extant version of The Primary Chronicle. Despite its age, it's not necessarily the most accurate regarding textual fidelity. Its significance is further heightened by being the sole source conveying the comprehensive works of Vladimir II Monomakh, including his teachings, autobiography, and correspondence with Oleg Sviatoslavich.

Named after its one-time owner, Prince Janusz Radziwiłł, a prominent figure from the Polish-Lithuanian noble class, the Radzivil Chronicle was gifted to the library of Königsberg Castle in 1668, earning it the alternate title of the Königsberg Copy. After the capture of Königsberg during the Seven Years' War, it was transported to Saint Petersburg in 1761, where it resided. Dating back to the late 15th century, its first publication was in 1767.

The Academy Chronicle, historically linked to the Moscow Ecclesiastical Academy, mirrors the Radzivil Chronicle up to the year 1206, often providing superior textual variants and filling its omissions. It is dated to the late 15th century as well.

The Trinity Chronicle, related to the Laurentian, was once housed in the Trinity Monastery's library before being relocated to Moscow in the late 18th century. Although destroyed by fire in 1812, early 19th-century copies of its fragments persist.

Discovered by Karamzin in the Hypatian Monastery in Kostroma, the Hypatian Chronicle was transcribed in the early 15th century but only published in 1908.

Originating from the first quarter of the 16th century, the Khlebnikov Chronicle bears the name of its owner, Khlebnikov, a Kolomna merchant. Despite being a century younger than the Hypatian Chronicle, it frequently offers more reliable textual versions.

The Primary Chronicle sets forth its purpose in the introduction, aiming to chronicle the origins of the Rus' land and its initial rulers. In its initial sections—often referred to as the "prehistoric pages"—The Primary Chronicle delves into the early inhabitants of the territories that would become Rus'. It highlights these peoples' diversity and ancient customs, tracing their origins back to the aftermath of the great flood linking the Slavs to the descendants of Japheth. It further narrates how the Slavs settled along the Danube River before spreading to other regions.

The narrative then transitions to the introduction of annual chronologies, marking the commencement of stories detailing the formation of Rus', its interactions with neighboring entities, the accomplishments of its leaders, fraternal conflicts, and fierce battles against foes. Significant European historical moments, such as the Rus' conversion to Christianity facilitated by Byzantium, are thoroughly chronicled.

Blending legend with historical facts in The Primary Chronicle exemplifies the compilation's nature, making it sometimes challenging to separate fact from folklore. This characteristic, common in medieval historiography, doesn't diminish the Chronicle's significance. Instead, including legends, whether as tangents or interwoven with historical narratives, offers invaluable insights, potentially connecting to the oral traditions that existed in Rus' before the Christianization, the origins and specifics of which remain to be explored.

It's also crucial to acknowledge that The Primary Chronicle was composed within the monastic confines of the Kiev Monastery of the Caves by authors closely associated with the Church, around 120 years after Rus' officially embraced Christianity in 988. During the early 12th century, the Kievan state was actively shaping its political and religious stance, especially in relation to Byzantium, its formidable neighbor. The Chronicle reflects the ideology Kiev sought to propagate across Rus, advocating for Kiev's political and spiritual autonomy from Constantinople. Christianity was pivotal in this ideological framework, with religious literature thriving in Kiev. Narratives of numerous Russian saints' lives, preceding their separate hagiographies, are found within the Chronicle's pages, alongside detailed accounts related to the Monastery of the Caves, where the Chronicle originated, including its abbots, monks, and saints.

The Primary Chronicle is a vital document for understanding the pre-Christian beliefs of the East Slavs and the diverse ethnic groups that unified under Kievan Rus'. As is typical of medieval texts, The Primary Chronicle was penned by clergy members who viewed non-Christian beliefs with disdain. Despite the clerical authors' critical or dismissive tones towards paganism, the Chronicle provides a window into the non-Christian traditions of Rus, presenting material that remains of scholarly interest a millennium later.

SLAVIC PAGANISM

Slavic Native Faith, or as it is known in contemporary circles, Rodnovery and Slavic paganism, occupies a unique and quiet place within our modern world. This ancient belief system, hailing from the verdant forests and rolling hills of Slavic lands, speaks of a time when humanity and nature were inextricably linked, and divine presences inhabited every corner of the earth.

Slavic paganism is the umbrella term for the Slavic peoples' pre-Christian religious practices and beliefs. This spiritual framework is not a monolith but a constellation of beliefs, rituals, and deities, reflecting the diverse cultures and environments of the Slavic world. From the sunlit waters of the Baltic to the dense forests of the Balkans, each region contributed its hues to the Slavic spiritual palette, creating a rich and varied tradition that resonates with the vibrancy of life itself. It's essential to understand that Slavic people, stretching from the north to the south and from the east to the west, shared some common gods and practices. However, there was also significant variation and variety among them.

Rodnovery and Slavic Native Faith signify more than just a historical curiosity. They represent a revival, a rekindling of ancient fires in the modern age. Rodnovery restores these age-old practices, adapting them within the context of contemporary life while striving to remain faithful to their origins. It is a pathway that connects the present with the past, offering a sense of identity and belonging through the reclamation of heritage and tradition. The term "rodnovery" is derived from two Slavic roots - "rod" meaning "kin, family, birth" and "very" meaning "faith, belief." Thus, rodnovery literally translates to "faith/belief of the kin/ancestors."

At its core, Slavic paganism is characterized by polytheism, the worship of multiple deities, each governing aspects of the natural world and human existence. This pantheon includes gods of thunder, fertility, sun, and moon, reflecting the Slavs' deep reverence for the forces of nature and their understanding of the interconnectedness of all life.

Moreover, Slavic Native Faith encompasses many practices, from seasonal festivals that mark the cyclical nature of time to rituals aimed at ensuring prosperity, health, and protection.

Ancestor veneration plays a pivotal role, emphasizing the continuity between the living and the departed, ensuring that the wisdom of the past is not lost but honored and remembered.

In exploring the definition and scope of Slavic paganism, one encounters a worldview that is both ancient and relevant today. It offers insights into a way of life where balance, respect, and reverence for the natural world are ideals and essentials for the well-being of the community and the individual. As we move further into the essence of Rodnovery and Slavic Native Faith, we uncover the roots of Slavic spirituality and the timeless principles that can guide us in navigating the complexities of the modern world.

In the historical context, Slavic paganism begins in the shadows of prehistory, where oral traditions and archaeological findings hint at a society deeply attuned to the rhythms of the natural world. These early Slavs observed the dance of the seasons, the whispers of the forest, and the spirits dwelling within each river and mountain, developing a rich pantheon of gods and spirits to encapsulate the forces that governed their lives.

As centuries turned, the Slavic world found itself at the crossroads of emerging empires and migrating peoples, each encounter weaving new strands into the spiritual heritage of the Slavs. Yet, the core of Slavic paganism—a reverence for nature, the veneration of ancestors, and the worship of a multitude of deities—remained steadfast, a constant star in the ever-changing skies.

The forceful introduction of Christianity in the late 1st millennium marked a turning point in the history of Slavic spirituality. Missionaries and rulers alike saw the conversion of the Slavic peoples as both a spiritual mandate and a means of political consolidation. The ensuing centuries witnessed a slow, often turbulent transition, where pagan practices were either assimilated into the new Christian fabric or driven into the shadows, persisting in folk customs and seasonal celebrations.

Despite these pressures, the essence of Slavic paganism never truly faded. Hidden beneath the veneer of Christian saints and rituals, the ancient gods and practices continued to breathe, biding their time. The 20th century, with its upheavals and quests for identity, witnessed a resurgence of interest in these old paths, leading to the revival known as Rodnovery.

This reawakening is about resurrecting forgotten gods and reclaiming a heritage that speaks to the Slavic soul. It's a journey back to when humanity lived in harmony with the land, guided by nature's cycles and ancestors' wisdom. In this context, Slavic paganism and its modern expressions offer not just a glimpse into the past but a living tradition that continues to evolve, adapt, and inspire.

Slavic paganism's core fundamental beliefs and practices are a polytheistic belief structure, a pantheon rich with gods and goddesses overseeing various aspects of existence. Among these deities, figures like Perun, the thunder god, and Veles, the underworld, stand as pillars of the Slavic divine hierarchy. Perun, wielding lightning bolts and maintaining order, contrasts with Veles, who resides in the moist earth, embodying chaos. This dynamic interplay between order and chaos, heaven and earth, permeates Slavic mythology, reflecting the complexities of life itself.

In addition to Perun and Veles, the Slavic pantheon hosts a multitude of other deities, each associated with specific elements of the natural or social world. Svarog, the celestial smith, forges the sun each night anew; Mokosh, the goddess of fertility and protector of women, blesses the earth with abundance; while Dazhbog, the sun god, rides his fiery chariot across the sky, bringing light and life to the world.

Central to Slavic paganism are the rituals and celebrations that mark the changing seasons and significant life events. These practices, woven into the fabric of daily life, ensured harmony between the community and the divine. Seasonal festivals celebrate the cycle of birth, death, and rebirth, acknowledging the eternal dance of nature. For example, the spring festival of Maslenitsa bids farewell to winter and welcomes the rejuvenating power of the sun. At the same time, Kupala Night, a midsummer festivity, celebrates fertility, purity, and the joy of life.

Ancestors hold a revered place in Slavic pagan practice, with rituals dedicated to honoring the dead and ensuring their benevolence. These customs, deeply rooted in the belief in the continuity between the living and the departed, reinforce the people's communal bonds and collective memory.

Slavic paganism articulates a world where the divine is intimately connected to the rhythms of nature and the human experience through these beliefs and practices. This ancient spirituality, with its deities and rituals, continues to inspire and guide individuals seeking to reconnect with their heritage and the timeless cycles of the natural world. As we explore the key beliefs and practices of Slavic paganism, we uncover not just the spiritual dimensions of the Slavic peoples but also the universal themes of harmony, respect, and reverence for life that resonate across cultures and epochs.

This is just a preceding glimpse into Slavic paganism, with its deities, rituals, and seasonal celebrations barely scratching the surface of this rich and multifaceted spiritual tradition. The complexity and depth of Slavic paganism, interwoven with centuries of history, culture, and evolving practice, defy simple explanation or summary. To fully appreciate the intricacies of this belief system, one would need to invest countless hours in study, and even then, new layers and connections would likely emerge. With its ancient roots and contemporary resurgence, this faith embodies a profound and dynamic spiritual landscape that continues to captivate and grow in followers.

As we further understand this captivating spiritual tradition, the Primary Chronicle is a beacon of historical and religious significance. This seminal document offers a window into the soul of early Slavic civilization, chronicling the advent of Christianity and providing invaluable insights into the pagan practices and beliefs that predated this transformation. The Chronicle serves as a bridge between two worlds, capturing the momentous shift from paganism to Christianity and preserving, within its pages, echoes of the pre-Christian faith that shaped the Slavic identity.

The Primary Chronicle is a repository of cultural memory, safeguarding the remnants of Slavic pagan traditions amidst the tides of change. By detailing rituals, deities, and the interplay between pagan and emerging Christian beliefs, the Chronicle offers scholars and practitioners a foundation to rebuild and recontextualize Slavic paganism in the modern era. Its accounts, while viewed through the lens of its time, provide critical clues for reconstructing the ancient faith, offering glimpses into the spiritual life of the Slavic peoples before the widespread acceptance of Christianity.

In the following pages, we view the essence of Slavic

paganism, drawing upon The Primary Chronicle as a critical source. Through careful examination and interpretation of this historical text, we hope to illuminate the enduring legacy of Slavic pagan beliefs and practices. By weaving together the insights preserved in the Chronicle with contemporary scholarship and practice, we seek to offer a more nuanced and vibrant portrayal of this ancient faith, shedding light on its complexities and continuing relevance and growth in today's world.

Thus, our journey through The Primary Chronicle is a quest to reconnect with the spiritual heritage of the Slavic peoples. It is an endeavor to understand how ancient beliefs and rituals can inform and enrich modern expressions of Slavic paganism, bridging the past with the present in a living tradition that continues to evolve and inspire.

TRIBAL CUSTOMS IN SLAVIC SOCIETIES C/13-14

In the opening sections of the Primary Chronicle, the narrative focuses on the biblical tale of Noah and the great flood, positioning it as a foundational myth that elucidates the diverse origins of the world's peoples. However, this Christian framing swiftly gives way to an in-depth exploration of the inhabitants of 12th-century Rus', with a particular emphasis on the Slavic peoples, their neighboring tribes, and the intricate web of interrelations that bound them together. The chronicler catalogs the various Slavic tribes, delving into their interconnected histories and interactions, thus setting the stage for a better understanding of their societal structures and vibrant culture.

It is in Columns 13 and 14 that the Chronicle truly comes alive, unveiling a wealth of invaluable insights into the pre-Christian folk traditions and customs of these Slavic tribes. These passages offer a rare glimpse into the socio-cultural fabric of early Slavic life, revealing the complex practices surrounding societal events, such as the selection of life partners and the rituals associated with death and the afterlife.

The Poljane, or Polyane, tribe, renowned as the original settlers of the region that would one day evolve into the great city of Kiev, are portrayed with an air of reverence and piety, even as the chronicler acknowledges their pagan roots. Their social customs, characterized by a deeply ingrained sense of respect and modesty, particularly towards female family members, and their unique marital practices, where the bride is respectfully escorted to the groom's abode, starkly contrasting the customs of tribes like the Drevlians. The Drevlians, in turn, are depicted as leading a more "savage" lifestyle, lacking structured marriage customs and resorting to the abduction of women. This practice would have been abhorrent to the emerging Christian sensibilities of the time.

Similarly, the Radimici, Vjaticĭ, and Severjane tribes are characterized as forest-dwellers, living in harmony with the natural world but engaging in practices that the chronicler deems uncouth and "diabolical," such as the abduction of women during communal games, dances, and rituals. Yet, from the perspective of the Slavic Native Faith, these very practices may have held deep cultural or spiritual significance, perhaps rooted in ancient courtship rituals or symbolic reenactments of mythological narratives.

The Chronicle's detailed account of the funeral practices of these tribes, particularly the rituals of cremation and the subsequent collection and display of remains along roadsides, offers a tantalizing glimpse into the complex spiritual beliefs surrounding death and the afterlife within the pagan Slavic worldview. These rites, far from mere "savagery," as the chronicler suggests, were likely steeped in symbolic meaning and a profound reverence for the cyclical nature of existence – a testament to the enduring spirit of the Slavic Native Faith.

This first section we covered offers a vivid description that not only highlights the remarkable cultural power that existed among the Slavic tribes but also underscores the varying degrees of social organization and sophistication that characterized their societies. The chronicler's account, though undoubtedly colored by the emerging Christian worldview, inadvertently preserves an invaluable window into Slavic pagan culture, showcasing the resilience and adaptability of these ancient traditions in the face of the encroaching influence of the new faith.

Column. 13–14 - The Primary Chronicle

"The Poljane had the custom of their parents; they were affable and calm and modestly respectful before their daughters-in-law and sisters and before their mothers, and the daughters-in-law had great respect for their mothers-in-law and fathers-in-law. And they had as a marriage custom that the bridegroom did not go to fetch his bride, but she was brought to him by night, and the following morning they took to her what they gave her. And the Drevlians lived savagely, lived like cattle, killed each other, ate all kinds of filth, and there was no marriage between them, but they abducted virgins in the water. The Radimici, Vjatici, and Severjane had a shared custom: they lived in the forest like wild animals, eating all kinds of filth, and they spoke obscenities to each other in front of their parents and daughters-in-law and there was no marriage between them, but games between the villages, and they came together for the games, for the dances and for all types of diabolical songs, and there [the men] abducted the women; he who had arranged with one of them, as each man had two or three women. And if a person died, they arranged a funeral rite for him, and after

this, they made a great pyre and placed the body on this pyre and set fire to it, and after collecting the bones, they placed them in a small receptacle and set it on a post on the roads, as the Vjatici̇̆ do today. These were the customs of the Krivici̇̆ and the other pagans, who did not know the law of God but made a law unto themselves".

THE FIRST TREATY: PAGAN DIPLOMACY C/32

This excerpt encapsulates a pivotal moment in the history of Kievan Rus, highlighting the interplay between the pagan Rus' and the Christian Byzantine Empire during the treaty negotiations between Prince Oleg and Emperors Leon and Alexander. This event underscores the political understanding of the Rus' and offers a rich insight into their religious practices and beliefs.

The ceremonial aspects of the treaty signing are particularly striking. The Byzantine Emperors adhere to their Christian faith, swearing on the cross. At the same time, Oleg and his warriors invoke their own pantheon, swearing by their weapons and the Slavic gods: Perun, associated with thunder and warfare, and Veles, the deity of cattle and wealth. This distinction in oath-taking rituals vividly illustrates the coexistence of different religious paradigms. It highlights how integral pagan practices and deities were in the Rus' socio-political and spiritual life. It underscores the deep reverence for these deities, not just in personal beliefs but also in legitimizing political agreements and alliances.

The request for sails of precious cloth for the Rus' and muslin for the Slavs by Oleg is symbolic, perhaps indicative of the differing status or roles within these groups, or simply a display of the spoils of a successful negotiation. The act of hanging his shield on the doors of Constantinople is a bold testament to his triumph, serving as a physical marker of victory and dominance over a major power.

Overall, this column demonstrates the syncretism of political power and religious faith in the early medieval period. It reflects the importance of pagan rituals and symbols in statecraft and diplomacy for the Kievan Rus', offering a glimpse into how these practices were intertwined with their identity and how they navigated their relationship with the Christian world. This moment in history, therefore, serves as a key illustration of the persistence and influence of pre-Christian Slavic native faith in the face of expanding Christian influence.

Column. 32 - The Primary Chronicle

"The emperors Leon and Alexander signed the peace with Oleg. They undertook to pay tribute and swore an oath to each other: they [the emperors] kissed the cross, and Oleg and his men swore an oath by the Rus' religion and swore by their weapons, and by Perun, their god, and by Veles, the god of cattle, and ratified the peace. And Oleg said: "Sew sails of precious cloth for the Rus', and sails of muslin for the Slavs". And this was done. And he hung his shield on the doors to show his victory and he went to Constantinople."

THE SECOND TREATY: SWEARING BY THE SWORD C/33

These columns bring out one of our first looks into the oath between Christians and the Rus', which involves swearing by their weapons. It gained additional depth and historical context when linked to the second treaty between the Rus and Byzantium, signed in 912 (6420). This earlier treaty also mentions the Rus' swearing on their weapons, pointing to a longstanding tradition within Slavic Native culture and a practice shared by other Indo-European groups.

The repeated mention of this ritual in both treaties underscores its deep-rooted significance in the Slavic Native Faith society. Swearing on weapons, a practice echoed across various Indo-European cultures, suggests a broader cultural and historical context where weapons transcended their practical utility. They were imbued with a symbolic value, representing honor, personal and communal identity, and perhaps even a spiritual connection to the divine or the ancestral.

This practice reflects a world where Slavic Native Faith and its customs were not isolated aspects of the Rus' society but were integrated into their political and diplomatic engagements. The act of swearing on weapons in these high-stakes diplomatic agreements underscores the sacrosanct nature of such oaths, binding them to the honor and spiritual beliefs associated with these arms.

Moreover, the integration of this pagan ritual into treaties with a Christian empire like Byzantium highlights a period of religious syncretism and cultural exchange. The mutual respect for each other's swearing methods – the Rus' on their weapons and the Byzantines likely through Christian rites – indicates a diplomatic landscape where different religious and cultural practices were acknowledged and accommodated.

This syncretic approach to diplomacy and oath-taking reveals the complexity of the Rus' identity during this period. It illustrates how pre-Christian Slavic native faith and customs coexisted and interacted with the spreading influence of Christianity, creating a multifaceted system of beliefs and practices. The Rus' willingness to swear by their weapons, a practice resonant with pagan traditions, alongside Christian rituals, speaks to a society navigating the crossroads of old and new religious landscapes. These columns enrich the understanding of the early Rus' oaths, showcasing it as part of a continuum of cultural and spiritual practices that defined the Rus' during this transformative era.

Column. 33 - The Primary Chronicle

"Between the Christians and the Rus', swearing by their weapons with an inviolable oath, not only spoken but also written, to profess and ratify this friendship by the faith and by our religion."

THE LEGEND OF PRINCE OLEG: FATE AND PROPHECY.
C/38—39

The narrative of Prince Oleg's demise, chronicled here, is a blend of history, mythology, and faith that provides a profound insight into pre-Christian Slavic society's religious and cultural fabric. Recorded for the year 912, this legend stands alone within the chronicle, distinct from the surrounding narratives of Rus'-Greek diplomatic affairs.

This tale of Oleg's death, with striking similarities to Scandinavian sagas, points to a potential shared mythological heritage or mutual influences between the Slavic and Scandinavian cultures. The possibility that this legend was imported into Slavic lore underscores the dynamic exchange and amalgamation of myths across early medieval European cultures.

Oleg's reaction to the prophecy of his death—foretold to occur through his beloved horse—reveals the profound reverence and fear of the early Slavs towards prophecies and omens. His decision to avoid the horse altogether reflects a pervasive belief in destiny and the inexorable nature of fate, themes deeply rooted in various pagan belief systems. This belief is further emphasized when, years later, a fatal encounter with a serpent emerging from his horse's skull fulfills the prophecy in an unexpected twist. This ironic fulfillment highlights a core tenet of Slavic native faith: the inescapability of fate and the folly of attempting to outmaneuver predestined outcomes.

The narrative also delves into the tension between pagan and emerging Christian beliefs. The author's insertion of a digression on witchcraft and supernatural phenomena, derived from Hamartolos, following Oleg's death, underscores the conflict between traditional Slavic beliefs and orthodox Christian teachings. This reflects the broader cultural and religious transitions occurring during the period of the Chronicle's compilation.

Significant in the legend is the esteemed role of Volkhvs or seers within Slavic society. Volkhvs were believed to possess mystical powers, particularly the ability to predict the future. Far from being mere folklore figures, these individuals wielded substantial influence, with their predictions and interpretations shaping political decisions and societal norms. Their integral role in Oleg's court exemplifies the depth to which pagan beliefs and practices were woven into the sociopolitical fabric of the time.

The account of Oleg's burial in a mound further illuminates Slavic Native Faith funerary customs. These burial mounds, symbolizing honor and remembrance, reflect Slavic culture's deep respect for the deceased. The enduring presence of Oleg's mound signifies the lasting impact of these pagan customs, persisting even as Christianity began to gain a foothold in the region.

This section from the Primary Chronicle is more than a historical account; it's a window into the spiritual views of the pre-Christian Slavs. It sheds light on their perceptions of prophecy, fate, and the intersection of the natural and supernatural worlds, offering a unique perspective on the complexity of their belief systems and societal norms.

Column. 38-39 - The Primary Chronicle

"And Oleg lived and reigned in Kiev and was at peace with all countries. And autumn came and Oleg remembered his horse, which he had ordered to be fed without riding it. Once he had asked the enchanters and seers: "What will I die of?" And a seer answered him: "Prince! Your horse, whom you love and whom you ride, your death will come from him". Oleg was troubled by these words and said: "I will ride him no more, nor will I see him again".

And he ordered that he should be fed and not brought before him. And some years passed without his seeing him, until he went against the Greeks. And he returned to Kiev, and four years went by, and in the fifth year he remembered his horse, by whom the seers had foretold his death. And he called the head groom to him and asked: "Where is my horse whom I ordered to be fed and cared for?" And the groom replied: "He died". Oleg laughed and mocked the seer, saying: "The enchanters do not tell the truth, but all are lies: the horse is dead but I am still alive". And he ordered a horse to be saddled up for him: "So I can see his bones". And he came to the place where the bare bones lay, and the bare skull, and dismounting from the horse, he laughed, saying: "Was my death supposed to come from this skull?" And he stamped on the skull with his foot, and a serpent came out from the skull and bit him on the foot. And he fell ill and died. And all the people mourned him with great lamenting, and they took him and buried him on the mountain known as Ščekovica. His burial mound still exists today; it is called the mound of Oleg. And all the years of his reign numbered."

THE THIRD TREATY: PERUN'S HILL C47-48, 53 AND 54

The narrative of the third treaty between the Rus', led by Prince Igor, and Byzantium in 945 A.D. (6453), as recorded in the Primary Chronicle, offers a captivating glimpse into the Rus' evolving religious and cultural landscape during this formative period. This treaty, remarkable for its intricate oath-taking process, reflects the nuanced interplay of pagan and Christian beliefs within Rus' society and their diplomatic relations with the mighty Byzantine Empire.

The initial part of the oath, conducted in Byzantium without Igor's presence, underscores the diplomatic gravitas and the acknowledgment of the Rus as a formidable entity operating within the broader geopolitical context of the era, where Byzantium stood as a significant Christian power. The presence of Christians in the Rus delegation highlights the progression of Christianity's influence in the region, even as pagan beliefs retained a strong foothold.

This religious dichotomy is strikingly illustrated by the invocation of the Christian God and the pagan deity Perun, the supreme god of the Slavic pantheon associated with thunder, lightning, and war. The absence of Veles, another prominent deity, may signify shifts within the pagan religious hierarchy or evolving worship practices. The oppositional mention of these divine figures encapsulates the religious diversity and potential tensions within Rus' society as it grappled with the spread of Christianity.

The dire consequences threatened for breaking the oath, including death by one's own weapons and the inability to defend oneself with a shield, resonate profoundly with the martial culture and the symbolic significance of armaments in Rus' society. This aspect of the oath underscores the seriousness of such agreements. It reflects the prevailing belief systems where personal honor and destiny were intimately linked to one's weapons.

Moreover, the notion of becoming slaves in the afterlife for violating the treaty introduces a complex understanding of the afterlife and moral accountability, concepts that intersect both pagan and Christian ideologies. This shared belief in a consequential afterlife underscores a common understanding of morality and justice that transcended the particularities of individual religious doctrines.

Repeating the oath at various points within the treaty signifies its critical importance. At the same time, the detailed description of the oath-taking by Igor and his men, involving

Constantinople's ambassadors in Kiev, adds a ceremonial and formal dimension to this process, highlighting the ritualistic aspects integral to such agreements.

Notably, the mention of Igor and his men worshipping before the idol of Perun on a hill provides a fascinating glimpse into the religious practices predating the formal Christianization of the Rus' under Vladimir. This detail underscores the deep-rooted and widespread nature of pagan worship, showing that these practices were not only prevalent but also publicly and officially acknowledged, even during this religious transition.

This section of the Primary Chronicle again portrays the complex religious dynamics and ceremonial diplomacy of the Rus' in the mid-10th century, revealing a society in the midst of profound religious transformation, where Native Faith and Christian beliefs coexisted and interacted, shaping not only the spiritual but also the political and social fabric of the era.

Column. 47-48 & 53-54 - The Primary Chronicle

"And anyone in the country of the Rus who seeks to destroy this friendship, if they have received salvation, may they suffer the vengeance of Almighty God, be condemned to perdition in this world and in the next; and if they are unbaptized, may they

obtain no succor either from God or from Perun, may they not defend themselves with their own shields, and may they die by their own swords, arrows and other weapons, and be slaves in this world and in the next. And anyone who in our country should violate it, be they a prince or anyone else, baptized or unbaptized, may they not be succored by God, may they be a slave in this world and in the next, and may they be dismembered by their own weapon.

And the unbaptized Rus, who laid down their shields and their un- sheathed swords, and their armbands41 and all their other weapons, and who swear by all that is written on this parchment, which will be respected by Igor and by all the boyars and by all the people of the Rus' country for all the years of the future and forever.

And if any of the princes or the Rus people, be they Christian or non- Christian, should transgress what is written on this parchment, they deserve to die by their own weapon, and to be damned by God and by Perun for having broken their oath.

And more, the great Prince Igor will demonstrate

his goodness, and maintain all this friendship as is fitting, so that it should not be transgressed, while the sun continues to shine and while everyone remains standing, in the present time and in the future.

And the next morning, Igor called his ambassadors and went to the hill where Perun was. And they laid down their weapons and their shields and their gold, and Igor swore his oath, and his men, and all the Rus who were pagans. And the Rus Christians swore the oath in the church of Saint Elijah (…).".

RITUALS OF REVENGE AND FUNERARY TRADITIONS- C/55-57

The narrative of Princess Olga's calculated acts of vengeance against the Derevlians in 945 (6453), following the murder of her husband, Prince Igor, offers a captivating glimpse into the ancient funerary rites and societal norms of the Slavic Native Faith. While Olga's actions are driven by a desire for retribution, they also subtly reflect elements of these pre-Christian rituals, particularly in the aftermath of Igor's funeral ceremony.

The account begins with the traditional pagan funerary rite known as the trizna or tryzna, which is held in honor of Igor. This ceremony, largely undocumented in historical records, provides rare insights into the Slavic approach to death and commemoration. The gathering of warriors at the trizna emphasizes Slavic society's communal and hierarchical nature, where such assemblies served to reinforce social bonds, express collective grief, and acknowledge the deceased's status and role within the community.

The consumption of alcohol to excess during the ceremony might have been a ceremonial practice to facilitate a shared sense of loss, a temporary release from societal norms, or perhaps a means to connect with the spiritual realm. The construction of a burial mound over Igor's tomb, a common practice across various Indo-European cultures, was not merely a grave but a monument symbolizing the deceased's status and serving as a lasting tribute, reflecting the deep respect for the dead and a belief in commemorating them through enduring physical markers.

Olga's active participation in mourning Igor highlights the role of women in these funerary rites. Her grief, while personal, also fulfilled a ritual obligation, showcasing the impact of loss on the family and the broader community. Her expression of sorrow, therefore, might have been a critical component of the ritual, intertwining personal emotion with communal tradition.

In this context of ancient funerary practices, Olga's calculated acts of revenge unfold. Her deceitful luring and brutal killing of the Derevlian emissaries, first by burying them alive and then by burning the nobles in a bathhouse, bear striking resemblances to the pagan Slavic reverence for fire as a purifying and transformative element, and the ritual sacrifices associated with the chthonic deities of the underworld.

Olga's cunning and ruthlessness in exacting vengeance

could be interpreted as a manifestation of the warrior spirit that permeated the pagan Slavic culture, where courage, strength, and cunning were highly prized. Her actions, while driven by personal vendetta, also reflect the societal norms and practices of her time, where rituals of death could intermingle with acts of retribution and justice.

The complex and nuanced picture of pre-Christian Slavic society provides insights into their rituals surrounding death, the societal role of women, and the interplay between personal vendetta and communal traditions. Olga's revenge narrative, set against the backdrop of Igor's funerary rites, not only recounts a tale of personal retribution but also opens a window into the cultural and religious practices of death and commemoration in Slavic communities before the advent of Christianity.

Column. 55-57 - The Primary Chronicle

"And they told Olga that the Drevlians were coming. And Olga called them before her and said: "Some delightful guests have arrived." And the Drevlians said: "We have arrived, princess." And Olga said to them: "Tell me then, what is your reason for coming?" And the Drevlians said: "We have been sent by the Drevlians land saying thus:

"We have killed your husband because your husband was like a wolf, sacking and plundering. But our princes are good, as they have brought peace to the Drevlians land. Marry our prince, marry Mal, as the prince of the Drevlians was called Mal"." And Olga said to them: "Your words are very pleasing to me, as I cannot resuscitate my husband. Tomorrow I wish to honor you before my people; go now to your boat and go to sleep and be exalted. Tomorrow I will go and fetch you, and you will say: 'We will go neither on horseback nor on foot, but you must take us by boat'. And they will bring you in the boat". And she let them go to the boat. Olga ordered a large deep pit to be built in the palace courtyard outside the city, and the next morning Olga, when she was at the palace, sent for the guests. And they went before them and said to them: "Olga calls you for a great honor". They answered: 'We will go neither on horseback, nor by cart, nor on foot, but you must take us by boat'. And the Keevan's said: "We have no choice: our prince is dead and our princess wishes to marry your prince", and they took them in the boat. And they took their places ostentatiously, proud of their large brooches on their breasts. And they took them to the palace before Olga and once they had taken them there, they threw them into the pit along with the boat. And bowing down, Olga asked them: "Did you find the honor pleasant?" They said: "It is worse than the death of Igor". And she ordered them to be buried alive, and they buried them.

Olga sent [a message] to the Drevlians and said: "If you really want to court me, send me distinguished men so I can marry your prince with great honors; otherwise, the people of Kiev will not let me go". Hearing this, the Drevlians chose the noblemen that governed the Drevlians land and send them to fetch her. Once the Drevlians had arrived, Olga ordered the bathhouse to be prepared, saying: "When you have washed, come before me". And they heated the bath, and the Drevlians entered and began to wash. And they closed the bathhouse behind them, and Olga ordered it to be set on fire from the doors, and they burned them all."

THE PAGAN OATHS OF SVJATOSLAV'S TREATY C/73

The oath recorded in the Primary Chronicle during the 971 (6479) peace treaty between Prince Svjatoslav of the Kievan Rus' and the Byzantine emperors serves as a powerful testament to the enduring relevance of the Slavic Native Faith within the realms of diplomacy and statecraft. This historical account offers a captivating window into the intricate interplay between religious traditions and diplomatic practices that characterized the Rus' society during this profound cultural and spiritual transformation period.

Svjatoslav's invocation of the pagan deities Perun and Veles as divine guarantors of the treaty with the Christian Byzantine Empire is a striking representation of the era's religious pluralism and syncretism. The mention of Perun, the supreme god of the Slavic pantheon associated with thunder, war, and justice, and Veles, the deity of cattle, wealth, and the underworld, within the solemn oath, underscores the enduring veneration of these ancient beliefs among the Rus' people, even as the influence of Christianity continued to spread.

The specific nature of the curse invoked for violating the

treaty – the threat of turning "yellow like gold" and being "dismembered by our own weapons" – reveals the profound belief in divine retribution and the moral weight attached to such oaths within the pagan Slavic worldview. This vivid and symbolic curse is a powerful indicator of the deep-rooted conviction in the tangible consequences of breaking sacred vows, inextricably tied to the spiritual power of the gods.

Significantly, this treaty occurred during a period of immense religious and cultural transition for the Rus' as the process of Christianization gradually gained momentum. Yet, the adherence to pagan rituals and the invocation of ancient deities in such a critical diplomatic agreement illustrates the resilience and continued veneration of traditional beliefs and practices, even as the new faith sought to establish its foothold.

Svjatoslav's decision to incorporate a pagan oath in negotiations with the Christian Byzantine Empire speaks volumes about the pragmatic approach to diplomacy that characterized the Rus' leadership. It reflects a society adeptly navigating the crossroads of old and new religious landscapes, where pagan and Christian elements intertwined within the social and political fabric, each finding its place within the evolving world.

Furthermore, respecting and integrating different cultural and religious identities within diplomatic relations demonstrates a remarkable degree of diplomatic tact and cultural sensitivity. It showcases an approach rooted in pragmatism and mutual understanding, where religious differences were acknowledged but did not impede the formation of strategic alliances and agreements.

The Primary Chronicle's account of this pagan oath in the 971 peace treaty offers a fascinating glimpse into the complex role played by the pre-Christian Slavic Native Faith during a time of significant religious and cultural transformation. It highlights the coexistence of pagan and Christian beliefs within the realm of diplomacy, reflecting a period of religious syncretism and the enduring influence of traditional Slavic religious practices within the very fabric of Rus' society.

Column. 73 - The Primary Chronicle

"And as I have sworn before the Greek emperors, and with me the boyars and all the Rus', we will respect the fair treaty. If we do not respect any part of the above, then may I and all those who are with me and under my power be damned by the gods in whom we believe Perun and Veles, the god of cattle, and let us turn yellow like gold, and be dismembered by our own weapons."

THE SLAVIC DEITIES, SACRIFICES, AND IDOLS HILL.

C/79

This excerpt from the Primary Chronicle is indeed considered one of the most significant written accounts detailing the practices and beliefs of the Slavic Native Faith during the pivotal period in Kievan Rus' under the rule of Prince Vladimir before the official adoption of Christianity. It offers an unparalleled glimpse into the vibrant world of pagan worship, shedding light on the intricate pantheon of deities and the rituals associated with their reverence.

The passage vividly describes Vladimir's establishment of a pagan sanctuary on a hill outside the palace in Kiev, where he erected idols representing various deities of the Slavic pantheon. Foremost among these was the idol of Perun, the supreme god of thunder, war, and justice, depicted with a wooden body adorned with a silver head and a gold mustache – a testament to the reverence accorded to this principal deity.

In addition to Perun, the account mentions the idols of Khors, Dazhbog, Stribog, Simargl, and Mokoš, each associated with distinct aspects of the natural world and human existence within the Slavic belief system. This diverse array of deities, myths, symbols, and spiritual associations formed the bedrock of the Slavic Native Faith.

The chronicle's description of sacrificial offerings, including the harrowing mention of human sacrifice, to these idols underscores the profound significance of such rituals within the pagan belief system. While the practice of human sacrifice remains a subject of scholarly debate, its inclusion in the account suggests that it was either an actual ritual or, at the very least, a deeply ingrained part of the collective memory and mythology of the Slavic people.

The chronicler's condemnation of these practices as "profaning the earth" and staining the hill with blood reflects the inherent Christian bias and the effort to vilify the pagan traditions as "devilish" in the face of the encroaching new faith. Yet, this very condemnation inadvertently preserves a precious record of the rituals and beliefs that governed the spiritual lives of the Rus' people for centuries before the advent of Christianity.

The subsequent mention of the Church of Saint Vasilij being erected on the same hill serves as a powerful symbolic representation of the supplanting of the pagan spiritual legacy by Christian symbolism and worship, marking a pivotal shift in the religious landscape of Kievan Rus'.

Furthermore, the account of Vladimir's uncle Dobrynja installing an idol beside the River Volkhov in Novgorod and demanding sacrifices from the inhabitants reinforces the widespread nature of pagan worship and the centrality of these rituals in the daily lives of the Slavic tribes across the Rus' territories.

This passage from the Primary Chronicle stands as a testament to the enduring legacy of the Slavic Native Faith, offering a rare and invaluable window into the deities, rituals, and spiritual beliefs that shaped the cultural and religious landscape of Kievan Rus' before the eventual transition to Christianity. It serves as a powerful reminder of the resilience and vibrancy of the pagan traditions that once held sway over the region and their profound influence on the Slavic peoples' beliefs, practices, and worldviews.

Column. 79 - The Primary Chronicle

"And Vladimir began to reign alone in Kiev. And he placed idols on the hill outside the palace: a Perun in wood with a silver head and a gold mustache, and Khors and Daždbog and Stribog and Simargl and Mokosh. And they offered sacrifices and called them gods, and they took their sons and daughters to them and sacrificed them to the devils. And they profaned

the earth with their sacrifices, and Rus' and that hill were profaned by blood. But God the merciful, who does not wish the death of sinners, on that hill stands today the church of Saint Vasilij, as we will relate later. But let us return to our previous matter. Vladimir installed his uncle Dobrynja in Novgorod. And when Dobrynja arrived in Novgorod, he placed an idol beside the River Volkhov, and offered the inhabitants of Novgorod as victims, as to a god".

THE CLASH OF FAITHS: PAGAN RESISTANCE C/82-83

This powerful passage from the Primary Chronicle, set during Vladimir's reign in 983 (6491), offers a nuanced and complex portrayal of the religious dynamics that characterized Kievan Rus' during this pivotal period. The narrative highlights the profound tensions and conflicts that arose as the ancient Slavic Native Faith, with its deeply entrenched pagan rituals and beliefs, encountered the growing influence of the emerging Christian faith.

The account centers around the harrowing episode of human sacrifice, a ritual steeped in the pagan traditions of the pre-Christian Slavic societies. The communal nature of this practice is underscored by the drawing of lots to select a sacrificial victim, be it a young man or a young woman. This process emphasizes these rituals' perceived collective importance and significance within the wider community.

However, the focus on a Varangian Christian family illuminates the complex religious dynamics in Kievan Rus'. The presence of this family, with their differing beliefs and unwavering adherence to the Christian faith, reflects the vibrant religious variety within the region during this period of profound transition. Their defiant refusal to surrender their son as a sacrificial offering to the Slavic pagan deities marks a significant ideological and spiritual clash between the ancient traditions and the encroaching new faith.

The Varangian father's passionate rejection of the pagan idols as mere "wooden figures" and his emotional affirmation of the monotheistic Christian God are a powerful testament to the growing ideological divide between the old and the new belief systems. Even in the face of grave danger, his unwavering stance foreshadows the eventual supplanting of the pagan traditions by the new religion.

Yet, the chronicle's portrayal of the violent reaction of the pagan community, culminating in the brutal murder of the Varangian father and son, underscores the depth of resistance and the severe societal repercussions that accompanied any challenge to the entrenched religious norms. This harrowing episode captures the conflict between paganism and Christianity and reveals the complex societal tensions and upheavals that inevitably accompany such profound religious transformations.

While the chronicler's framing of this narrative, with its dramatic and poignant elements, undoubtedly serves to emphasize the perceived moral and spiritual superiority of Christianity over pagan beliefs, the historical accuracy of the specific details, particularly regarding the practice of human sacrifice within Slavic paganism, remains a subject of scholarly debate. Some historians suggest that such accounts may have been exaggerated or sensationalized, serving as a narrative strategy to draw stark contrasts between the "barbaric" pagan customs and the "civilized" Christian practices, promoting the new faith while diminishing the ancient pagan heritage.

Nonetheless, this excerpt from the Primary Chronicle stands as a powerful testament to the tumultuous religious landscape of Kievan Rus' during Vladimir's reign. It offers a vivid glimpse into the challenges faced by the ancient pagan rituals and traditions as they encountered the relentless spread of Christianity, showcasing the intricate interplay of faith, tradition, and societal change that characterized this pivotal period in the region's history.

Column. 82-83 - The Primary Chronicle

"And (Vladimir) went to Kiev, and made a sacrifice to the idols with their people. And the elders and the boyars said: "Let us draw lots between a young man and a girl, and whoever is chosen, we will sacrifice them to the gods". There was then a Varangian, and his estate was where today stands the temple of the Holy Mother of God built by

Vladimir. This Varangian had arrived from Byzantium and professed the Christian faith, and he had a son who was attractive both in his visage and his soul. And it was his misfortune to be envied by the devil, as the devil could not countenance him because having power over everyone, this man was for him like a thorn in his heart, and the evil one sought his downfall and to incite people against him. And those that were sent to him arrived and said to him: "Your son has been lucky, the gods have chosen him for themselves, so we can offer a sacrifice to the gods". And the Varangian said: "These are not gods but simply wood; today they exist but tomorrow they will disappear. They do not eat, they do not drink, and they do not speak, but they are made of wood by men's hands. There is only one God, who is served and venerated by the Greeks, the God who created heaven and earth, and the stars and the moon and the sun and man, and allowed him to live on the earth. And what have these gods done? They themselves have been made. I will not deliver my son to the demons". The emissaries went away and told the people. Taking up their arms, they went to where he lived and they destroyed the estate all around it. He was standing in the covered gallery with his son. They said to him: "Give us your son so we can deliver him to the gods". But he said: "If they are gods, they should send one of their own to take my son; but you, why do you need him?" And they gave a cry and demolished the gallery from below, and that way they killed them. And no one knows where they were buried because the people at that time were ignorant and pagan.".

VLADIMIR'S CONVERSION: THE FALL OF THE IDOLS C/116-117

The passage recounting Vladimir's forceful destruction of the idols representing the deities of the Slavic Native Faith in 988 (6496) takes on profound significance when viewed within the context of the transformative events that marked his reign, particularly his personal conversion to Christianity and his marriage to the Byzantine princess Anna.

In 988, following his military conquest of Cherson and subsequent embrace of the Christian faith, Vladimir's personal and political life underwent a seismic shift. His marriage to Anna, the sister of the Byzantine emperor's Basil and Constantine, was not merely a diplomatic alliance but a symbolic event that marked a pivotal turning point in the religious trajectory of Kievan Rus'. This union represented a deepening of ties between the Kievan state and the Byzantine Empire, both on the political and spiritual fronts.

Vladimir's return to Kiev with his newly-wed Byzantine wife and a retinue that included Christian priests bearing sacred relics clearly signals his unwavering commitment to his newfound faith. His decision to demolish the very pantheon of Slavic Native Faith idols that he had erected just eight years prior was a radical and profoundly symbolic act, signifying the official end of the ruling pagan cult in Kievan Rus'. This act transcended the mere physical destruction of idols; it represented a profound shift in the cultural and religious identity of the realm.

The desecration of the idols, particularly the dramatic and humiliating treatment meted out to the idol of Perun, the supreme deity of the Slavic pantheon, was a deliberate and calculated act intended to demonstrate the perceived violence and superiority of Christianity over the traditional Slavic beliefs. The act of tying Perun's idol to a horse's tail, dragging it through the streets, and subjecting it to beatings by twelve men was a powerful symbolic gesture designed to humiliate and desacralize the deity and its followers. This spectacle served as a potent message to the people of Kievan Rus about the impotence of their old gods in the face of the might of the Christian God.

The poignant reaction of the non-believers, who wept and mourned the destruction of their sacred idols, shows us the profound emotional and spiritual connection that bound the Slavic people to their native beliefs. This scene captures the complexities and challenges accompanying the forceful transformation of religious identity, illustrating that the shift from the Slavic Native Faith to Christianity involved significant emotional and cultural upheaval, not merely a change in spiritual practices.

The broader historical context of these events, particularly Vladimir's political maneuverings and his strategic use of religion as a tool for statecraft, adds layers of nuance and complexity to the narrative. It underscores the intricate interplay between faith, politics, and cultural transformation that characterized this pivotal period in the history of Kievan Rus'.

This telling account of Vladimir's destruction of the pagan idols, set against the backdrop of his personal conversion to Christianity and the political consolidation of his reign, symbolizes a defining moment in the history of Kievan Rus'. It represents the transition from a society rooted in traditional native faith to a Christian vassal state, inextricably linked to the Byzantine Empire through the bonds of religion and diplomacy. This passage encapsulates the intricate interplay of faith, politics, and cultural upheaval that shaped the destiny of the Kievan realm during this transformative era.

Column. 116-117 - The Primary Chronicle

"And when he arrived, he ordered the idols to be demolished, smashing some of them into pieces and throwing others into the fire. He ordered Perun to be tied to a horse's tail and dragged downhill along the Borichev slope to the Rukhai, and he placed 12 men so they could beat him with sticks, not because wood can feel anything, but to humiliate the devil, who had deceived the people with this image, and so the people could be avenged. "You are great, oh Lord, and your deeds are miraculous!" Yesterday he was honoured by the people, and now we insult him. When they dragged him along the Rukhai to the Dnieper the non-believers wept, as they had not yet been baptised. And having dragged him they threw him into the Dnieper. And Vladimir commanded, saying: "If he runs aground somewhere, push him far from the shore until he has passed the rapids; then you can let him go". They did as he ordered. When they let him go, he crossed the rapids, and the wind blew him onto a sandbank, which to the present day is known as the Perun sandbank.".

VLADIMIR'S FINAL JOURNEY: BURIAL AND TRADITION
C/140

As detailed in column 140, the account of Prince Vladimir's burial in 1015 (6123) takes on profound layers of significance when viewed through the lens of the specific practices and beliefs surrounding death and interment within the Slavic Native Faith traditions. These nuanced insights not only underscore the intricate syncretism of Christian and pagan elements but also reveal the enduring influence of the ancient Slavic beliefs during this transformative period in the religious landscape of Kievan Rus'.

Vladimir's death marked a pivotal moment, not merely in the political realm but also in the ongoing evolution of the region's religious identity. The method employed in handling his body for burial, particularly the custom of removing the deceased through a specially constructed hole or window, is deeply rooted in ancient pagan traditions. This practice was believed to disorient the soul of the departed, preventing it from returning to the earthly realm as a malignant spirit or vampire – a belief that speaks to the notions surrounding the nature of the soul, death, and the afterlife.

Yet, the decision to inter Vladimir's remains within the hallowed confines of the Church of the Holy Mother of God, a symbol of his legacy as the ruler who ushered in the Christianization of the realm, stands in stark contrast to these pagan burial practices. This juxtaposition underscores the complex and multifaceted religious identity that characterized Kievan Rus' during this era of profound transition.

The elaborate mourning process described in the account, involving widespread grief and lamentations from all strata of society, further illustrates the intricate blending of religious and cultural traditions. The noble elite boyars mourned Vladimir as the "protector of their country." At the same time, the common folk wept for him as their "protector and provider" – roles deeply ingrained in the Slavic societal structure and resonant with the pagan notions of leadership, community, and reverence for authority.

The use of a grand marble tomb, a feature more closely aligned with Christian burial traditions, alongside the secretive and ritualistic handling of Vladimir's body, reflects a society caught in the throes of religious change and transformation. This convergence of elements showcases the nuanced intermingling of the new Christian beliefs with the longstanding pagan customs, particularly those concerning the rituals and beliefs surrounding death and the treatment of the deceased.

This portrayal of Vladimir's burial is, enriched by the contextual understanding of the Slavic pagan customs and beliefs surrounding death, and gives us a picture of a society navigating the crossroads of old and new faiths. It is a rare and invaluable glimpse into the complexities of religious transition, showing how the Christian and Slavic Pagan beliefs coexisted, interacted, and influenced one another during this period of cultural and spiritual upheaval in early 11th-century Kievan Rus'.

Column. 140 - The Primary Chronicle

"By night, opening a hole in the ground between (two) chambers, and wrapping it in a carpet, they lowered him into the ground with some ropes; and laying him on a sled, and taking him with them, they placed him in the church of the Holy Mother of God which he himself had built. When the people found out, a large number gathered and wept for him: the boyars as the protector of their country, the poor people as their protector and their provider. And they put him in a marble sepulchre, and buried the body of the blessed prince with weeping.".

SORCERERS' UPRISING AND RELIGIOUS TENSIONS, C/147-148

As chronicled, the events of 1024 (6532) cast a revealing light on the societal and religious landscape of Kievan Rus', particularly in the aftermath of Prince ladimir's death and the Christianization of the state. This period was defined by the shift from paganism to Christianity and significant social and political unrest, as evidenced by the famine-induced uprising led by sorcerers or Volkhvs.

The uprising of 1024, driven by a severe famine, highlights the lingering influence and respect for Slavic Native Faith beliefs and practices. The leadership role of sorcerers or volkhv in this rebellion against the Rurikid dynasty, the ruling family in Rus', underscores these figures' enduring power and societal relevance. Despite the official adoption of Christianity under Vladimir, these practitioners of magic, rooted in pagan traditions, retained significant influence among the populace. Their ability to lead a popular uprising suggests a deep-seated connection and allegiance of the people to their native beliefs, particularly in times of crisis.

The uprising's origins, portrayed as a desperate act of the common folk driven to desperation by famine, cast the volkhv as protectors of the people, seeking to preserve the ancient wisdom and traditions that had sustained their ancestors for generations. The chronicler's depiction of their actions as inspired by the "devil" reflects the Christian bias against the old ways, which were deeply rooted in the spiritual practices and rituals of the Slavic Native Faith.

The subsequent departure of the people to Bulgaria, where they sought sustenance and refuge, underscores the profound upheaval caused by the imposition of the new faith and the disruption of traditional ways of life. The people, torn between the ancient beliefs and the foreign religion, were forced to abandon their homes and seek solace in lands where the old gods still held sway, highlighting the resilience of pagan traditions.

The final act of Yaroslav, the Christian prince, in brutally suppressing the uprising and executing the volkhv, is a testament to the violent oppression faced by the adherents of the Slavic Native Faith. The author's sympathies lie with these martyrs, who are depicted as defenders of the ancient beliefs that had sustained the Slavic peoples for centuries.

The uprising of 1024 reveals the resilience of pagan traditions and the challenges faced by the newly established

Christian order. It illustrates the tensions between the ruling dynasty, which had embraced Christianity, and sections of the populace still holding onto their pagan roots. This tension was not just religious but also political, as it intersected with broader issues of governance, social justice, and response to crises like famine. The author's bias shines through, offering a glimpse into the tumultuous period when the old ways clashed with the new, and the Slavic people fought to preserve their cultural identity in the face of religious upheaval.

Column. 147-148- The Primary Chronicle

"That same year, there was an uprising of sorcerers in Suzdál'; they killed the old people under instruction and inspired by the devil, saying "They are keeping the reserves". And there was a great revolt and famine throughout the entire region, and all the people went along the Volga to Bulgaria and gathered grain and that way they survived. Hearing of the sorcerers, Yaroslav went to Suzdál', seized and scattered the sorcerers, and executed others.".

VSESLAV BIRTH PHENOMENA, C/155

The narrative of Vseslav Bryachislavich's birth in 1029) is a striking example of the persistence and influence of Native Faith beliefs and practices. Vseslav's birth, marked by the presence of an amniotic membrane on his head, is imbued with deep cultural and mystical significance. Such birth phenomena were often interpreted as omens or signs of a unique destiny in various cultures. This would have been a potent symbol in the context of Slavic paganism. It likely marked Vseslav as someone destined for a unique path linked to the supernatural or mystical realms. This belief is reinforced by Vseslav's association with the legendary figure Volkh Vseslavich, known for his magical abilities, suggesting a blend of historical and mythological narratives in his characterization.

The role of the volkhv (sorcerers) in Vseslav's story is particularly telling. They were present at the royal court and played an influential advisory role. This indicates that, despite the Christianization of the state, pagan beliefs and practitioners held a significant place in the royal court and the societal hierarchy. The advice these volkhv gave to Vseslav's mother about the amniotic membrane signifies a continued reliance on and reverence for pagan wisdom and practices, especially in matters considered to be influenced by otherworldly forces.

The author's reverence for the ancient Slavic beliefs is evident in the portrayal of the volkhvy's guidance as sacrosanct, with the implication that Vseslav's renowned mercilessness and propensity for spilling blood are directly linked to his adherence to this pagan ritual. This attribution of martial prowess and ruthlessness to the preservation of the sacred membrane starkly contrasts the Christian ideals of mercy and compassion, underscoring the author's allegiance to the ancient ways.

Furthermore, the fact that this account is mentioned several decades after the Christianization of Kievan Rus highlights the slow and complex process of religious transformation. It suggests that the transition to Christianity was not a straightforward replacement of one set of beliefs with another but rather a gradual and syncretic blending of new and old traditions. The author's emphasis on Vseslav carrying the membrane "to the present day" highlights the enduring influence of the Slavic Native Faith and its practices, even in the face of the new religion's spread.

Column. 155 - The Primary Chronicle

"(...) And Vseslav, his son, sat on his throne. His mother had given birth to him with magic: as when his mother gave birth to him, he had a membrane on his head. The sorcerers said to his mother: "Attach the membrane to his head so he carries it all his life", and Vseslav carries it to the present day; this is why he is merciless when spilling blood.".

THE NOMADIC INVASION AND THE RUSALIAS, C/170

The passage from 1068 (6576) in the Primary Chronicle again offers a glimpse into the enduring presence of pagan beliefs and practices among the populace of Kievan Rus' despite the official adoption of Christianity. While the author condemns these customs as "pagan" and attributes them to the workings of the devil, their very mention highlights the resilience of the Slavic Native Faith traditions in the face of the new religion's encroachment.

The author's lament that "we live as pagans" betrays the stubborn persistence of these ancient beliefs and rituals among the people. The reference to turning around upon encountering certain animals or figures speaks to the deep-rooted superstitions and omens that were woven into the fabric of daily life, echoing the reverence for the natural world that was a hallmark of the Slavic pagan worldview.

The mention of the belief in sneezing as a sign of good health offers a glimpse into the rich folk wisdom and traditions passed down through generations, far from being mere "temptations of the devil," as the author suggests. Similarly, the author's condemnation of the Rusalias – a pagan festival honoring the spirits of nature – betrays a fundamental misunderstanding, or perhaps a willful ignorance, of the profound spiritual significance these celebrations held for the adherents of the Slavic Native Faith.

The author's description of the "games assembled" and the crowds "pressing against each other" reveals a deep-seated aversion to the communal and exuberant nature of these pagan festivities. However, to the adherents of the Slavic Native Faith, these gatherings were not mere "games" but somewhat sacred rituals and celebrations that bound communities together and reinforced their connection to the natural world and the ancient traditions of their ancestors.

The events of 1068, interpreted by the Christian chronicler as divine retribution for the impiety of the Rus' inhabitants and their adherence to pagan customs, offer a glimpse into the intricate relationship between Christianity and the enduring pagan beliefs during this period of religious transition. While the chronicler's perspective is undoubtedly shaped by a Christian worldview, their reflections inadvertently shed light on the resilience and popularity of the Slavic Native Faith among the people.

The persistence of practices related to omens, superstitions, and traditional festivals points to a deep-seated cultural continuity, where these pagan traditions continued to thrive despite the official embrace of Christianity. The mention of specific customs, such as turning around upon encountering certain figures or animals, attaching significance to sneezing, and participating in festivities honoring the water spirits Rusalias, underscores the challenge faced by the Christian church in supplanting these long-held beliefs.

Through this passage, we glimpse the struggle between the old ways and the new, as the adherents of the Slavic Native Faith fought to preserve their cherished traditions and worldview in the face of the encroaching tide of Christianity. The coexistence of Christian and pagan elements in the people's daily lives highlights the syncretic nature of religious practices in Kievan Rus' during this tumultuous transition period.

Column. 170- The Primary Chronicle

"So do we not live as pagans if we believe in encounters? When someone meets a monk, or a wild boar or a sow they turn around: is this not pagan? Under instruction from the devil, they thus believe in omens; others believe in sneezing, which occurs for the health of the head. But the devil tempts us with these things and in other ways, distancing us from God with all the temptations, with trumpets and with minstrels and with guslis and with Rusalias. We see the games assembled, and many people in them, and they begin to press against each other and see things that have been thought up by the devil.".

SORCERY IN 1071 KIEVAN RUS, C/174—175

The narrative of the sorcerer's unfulfilled prophecy in 1071 (6579), as depicted, provides additional context to the ongoing presence and influence of sorcerers in Kievan Rus', even as Christianity continued to solidify its hold. This account and other mentions of sorcerers from the same period highlight the enduring popularity and significance of these figures operating outside Christian orthodoxy.

In 1071, the chronicler described the case of a sorcerer who made a dramatic prophecy about the reversal of the Dnieper River's flow and the geographical swapping of lands. The fact that this prophecy never came to fruition is less important than the attention it garnered among the people of Kiev. The populace's reaction, with some being skeptical and others more credulous, underscores the divided beliefs of the time. While the Christian community dismissed the prophecy as demonic deception, others, possibly still influenced by or adherent to pagan traditions, were more inclined to believe or at least listen to the sorcerer.

The inclusion of this and other accounts of sorcerers in the

Chronicle is a testament to the popularity these figures enjoyed, even outside orthodox Christian circles. Sorcerers, often seen as holy men or wise figures in Native Faith traditions, played crucial roles in interpreting omens, making predictions, and providing guidance based on their perceived connections with the divine or supernatural realms. Their continued presence and the attention they received indicate that pagan beliefs and practices, particularly those involving magic and divination, still held sway among population segments.

This ongoing popularity of sorcerers reflects Kievan Rus's complex religious and cultural dynamics during this period. The persistence of Slavic Native Faith beliefs, especially those related to magic and the supernatural, highlights a society in a slow and multifaceted religious transition. While the Christian faith was increasingly dominant, the old pagan traditions and figures like sorcerers continued to influence and resonate with the people.

Column. 174-175 - The Primary Chronicle

"at that same time a sorcerer inveigled by a demon arrived; he came to Kiev saying: "Five gods have appeared to me and said this: 'Tell the people that in the fifth year the Dnieper will flow backwards and the countries will change place so that the Greek land will be where the Rus' land is and the Rus' land where the Greek land is, and the other countries will change place'". The simple people listened to him, but the believers laughed and said to him: "A demon is playing with you to lead you astray". And this was what happened, as one night he disappeared without a trace.".

SORCERY, REBELLION, AND RELIGIOUS SYNCRETISM, C/175-178

The chronicle's account of the 1071 (6579) rebellion led by two sorcerers from Yaroslavl in Beloozero offers a glimpse into the enduring influence of Slavic paganism and the complex of religious and cultural beliefs that coexisted in Kievan Rus' during this period. This tale not only underscores the power and reverence still accorded to these mystical figures but also reveals the rich syncretism and diversity that characterized the spiritual landscape of the time.

The sorcerers' actions, depicted as a rebellion against the ruling authorities, speak volumes about the significant sway they still held over the hearts and minds of the people. Their ability to amass a following and challenge the established order demonstrates the deep-rooted respect and influence that the practitioners of the ancient pagan traditions continued to wield, even as Christianity sought to supplant the old ways.

The author's depiction of the sorcerers' rituals, involving the "magical" cutting of noblewomen's shoulders and the extraction of various items, resonates with the rich symbolism and mystical practices underpinning the Slavic Native Faith. While the Christian chronicler portrays these acts as brutal and cruel, they may have been rooted in ancient rites and beliefs, misunderstood and vilified by the emerging religious orthodoxy.

Moreover, how the sorcerers executed their rituals, described as resembling a Mordvin ritual, reveals the intricate tapestry of cultural influences that shaped the spiritual landscape of Kievan Rus'. This syncretism of practices, potentially drawing from various indigenous traditions, underscores the diversity and fluidity of the beliefs and customs that coexisted within the region.

The sorcerers' legend about human creation, which aligns with the dualistic worldview of the Bogomils, further enriches our understanding of the religious complexity of the time. The presence of these beliefs, distinct from both the Slavic Native Faith and orthodox Christianity, suggests that Kievan Rus' was not merely a battleground between paganism and Christianity but was also influenced by other contemporary religious currents.

The community's response to the sorcerers, involving their execution and the subsequent desecration of their bodies by a bear, reflects the complex dynamics between the ancient pagan practices and the emerging Christian order. The retribution to the sorcerers was likely steeped in symbolic significance, reflecting the clash between the old and new belief systems.

Through this harrowing account, the author inadvertently highlights the resilience of the Slavic pagan beliefs and the rich tapestry of religious and cultural influences that shaped the spiritual landscape of Kievan Rus'. The sorcerers' defiance and enduring reverence for their mystical arts serve as a powerful testament to the stubbornness with which the ancient faith refused to be extinguished, even in the face of the rising tide of Christianity.

This narrative offers valuable insight into the complex and multifaceted religious transformation that was unfolding in Kievan Rus' during this period. It highlights a society where traditional pagan beliefs and practices coexisted and intermingled with emerging Christian doctrines and other contemporary religious ideas, shaping a unique and dynamic cultural and spiritual identity that defied simple categorization.

Column. 175-178 - The Primary Chronicle

"There was a famine in the region of Rostov, and two sorcerers from Jaroslavl' rose up, saying: "We two know who is hiding the reserves". And they went walking along the Volga, and when they came to a village, they gathered all the noblewomen together saying: "These women are hiding

cereals, and these ones are hiding honey, and these fish, and these furs". And they brought their sisters and mothers and wives before the two. They sliced through them in a magical way cutting them behind their shoulders, and they removed either cereals, or fish, (or squirrel furs), and killed many women, and kept their possessions. And they came to Beloozero, and there were another 300 people with them. At the same time it happened that Jan, son of Vyšata, arrived from Svjatoslav collecting tax, and the people of Beloozero told him that two sorcerers had already killed many women along the Volga and the Šeksna, and that they had arrived there. Jan asked whose countrymen they were, and, discovering that they were his own prince's, sent them before those who were with the two, and said to them: "Bring those two sorcerers here, as these are the countrymen of my prince". But they paid no heed to him. Jan was unarmed, and his men said to him: "Do not go without weapons, they will humiliate you". He ordered his men to take up their arms; and there were 12 men with him, and they went towards them to the wood. But they confronted him, ready for a fight. Jan went with an axe, three of them came forward, they came before Jan and said to him: "You are deliberately going towards death, do not go!" But he ordered them to be killed, and he went for the others. And they charged at Jan, one missed Jan with the axe, but Jan, turning the axe around, hit him with the edge (of the axe) and ordered his men to cut his throat. They escaped to the wood, and there they killed Jan's priest. Jan, entering the city where the people of Beloozero were, said to them: "I will not leave here the whole summer long unless you catch those two sorcerers".

And the people of Beloozero went and caught them and brought them to him. And he said to the two: "Why have you killed so many people?" And they said: "Because they are hiding the reserves, and if we rid ourselves of them, there will be abundance. If you want, we will extract cereals or fish or anything else before your eyes". But Jan said: "In truth, you are lying, as God created man on earth, he is made of bones and veins with blood, and there is nothing more in him, and he does not know anything, but only God knows". And they said: "We know how man was created". And he asked: "How?" The two of them said: "God was washing in a bathhouse, and he began to sweat, and he wiped himself with a cloth of herbs, and he threw it from heaven down to earth. And Satan began to argue with God about who would create man from it (the cloth). And the devil created man, but God put the soul in him. That is why, when a man dies, his body goes to earth and his soul to God". Jan said to them: "In truth you have been inveigled by a demon. Which god do you believe in?" They said: "In the Antichrist". And he asked them: "Where is he?" They answered: "He lives in the abyss". Jan said to them: "What god is that who lives in the abyss? That is a demon; God is in heaven seated on his throne, honored by the angels, who are before Him in fear and are unable to gaze on Him. One of these angels was expelled, the one you call the Antichrist, for his pride he was expelled from heaven, and he is in the abyss, as you say, waiting for God to come from heaven and seize that Antichrist, he binds him with chains and leaves him prisoner in the eternal fire with his servants and with those who believe in him. But you two are destined to suffer my torture here, and there after death". And they said: "The gods tell us that you cannot do any-thing to us". And he answered them: "Your gods are lying to you". And they said: "It is our fate to go before Svjatoslav, but you cannot do anything to us". And Jan ordered them to be beaten and their beards to be pulled out. After whipping them and pulling out their beards with one wrench, Jan said to them: "What do the gods say to you?" And they said: "It is our fate to go before Svjatoslav". And Jan commanded that a gag should be put in their mouths, and they should be tied to the mast, and the boat should be cast off in front of him, and he went behind them. And they stopped at the mouth of the Šeksna, and Jan said to them: "What do the gods say to you?" And they said: "This is what the gods say: that we will not remain alive because of you". And Jan said to them: "They have spoken the truth". And they said: "If you let us go free you will receive many good things, but if you kill us you will receive many misfortunes and evils". He said to them: "If I let you go evils will come from God; if I kill you I will be rewarded". And Jan said to the oarsmen: "Which of you has had a family member killed by these two?" They said: "My mother, my sister, my daughter". He said to them: "Avenge your womenfolk!" They seized them and killed them and hung them from an oak tree; with justice they suffered God's vengeance. After Jan had gone home, on the second night a bear climbed (the oak tree), tore them to pieces and devoured them. And that is how they died by the incitement of demons, knowing and thinking about others but without foreseeing their own downfall.".

CROSS-CULTURAL ENCOUNTERS IN MAGIC, C/179

The 1071 (6579) account of the Novgorod native consulting a Chud' sorcerer, as recorded, illustrates Kievan Rus' cultural and religious diversity and provides insight into the perception and interpretation of magical practices by contemporary Christian observers.

This story, involving the Finnish tribe of the Chud', extends the narrative scope beyond Slavic pagan practices, highlighting the ethnographic and cultural diversity within the region. Including a Finnish sorcerer's story in a predominantly Slavic-focused chronicle underscores the multifaceted nature of spiritual and magical practices in Rus' territory. It reflects a region where various ethnic groups, each with their unique spiritual beliefs and practices, coexisted and interacted.

The interaction between the Novgorod native and the Chud' sorcerer, particularly the impact of a Christian symbol (the cross) on their ritual, reveals a complex interplay of different religious beliefs. This encounter demonstrates how Christian and non-Christian faiths, including those from Finnish pagan traditions, coexisted, sometimes in conflict and other times in a syncretic blend.

From the perspective of the Christian chronicler, this account likely served to illustrate the power and authority of Christian symbols over pagan rituals. The disruption caused by the cross in the sorcerer's ritual can be seen as a symbolic representation of the Christian worldview prevailing over other spiritual practices. This interpretation reflects the chronicler's aim to demonstrate the superiority of Christianity, a common theme in Christian texts of the time.

Additionally, the sorcerer's explanation of the pagan gods and the afterlife, though not directly related to Slavic beliefs, offers a glimpse into how Christian authors perceived and conveyed non-Christian spiritual concepts. The chronicler's representation of these beliefs, filtered through a Christian lens, provides valuable insight into how Christian authorities of the time viewed and depicted non-Christian practices.

Through this encounter, the author inadvertently shines a light on the resilience of the Slavic pagan traditions and the enduring reverence for their mystical practitioners, even in the face of Christianity's encroachment. Despite the presence of the cross, the sorcerer's unwavering belief in his gods and his ability to communicate with them serves as a powerful testament to the stubbornness with which the ancient faith refused to be extinguished. The sorcerer's ritual and beliefs reflect the rich cultural heritage of the Slavic peoples. This heritage refused to be erased by the tide of Christianity, instead persisting and intermingling with the emerging religious orthodoxy.

Column. 179 - The Primary Chronicle

"As in this period, in those years, it happened that a native of Novgorod went to the place of the Cud', and went to a sorcerer in search of his magic. And as was his custom he began to call up the demons in his house. The native of Novgorod was sitting on the threshold of his home, and the sorcerer lay dazed, and the demon shook him; the sorcerer rose and said to the native of Novgorod: "The gods do not dare come; there is something in you that they fear." The native of Novgorod remembered he was carrying a cross, and he moved away and put it outside that house. The sorcerer began to call up the demons again; the demons, pushing him, told him why they had come; then he began to ask him: "Why are you afraid of this, of this cross that we carry on us?" And he said: "It is a symbol of the heavenly God and our gods fear him". He said: "So what kind of gods are yours? Where do they live?" He said: "Our gods live in the abysses. They are black, they have wings and tails; they rise under heaven, listening to your gods, as your gods are in heaven. And when one of your people dies, he is taken up to heaven; but when one of our people dies, then he is taken down to the abyss".

DEAD AMONG THE LIVING C/208

This brief passage from the Primary Chronicle shows the disdain and suspicion that the adherents of the ancient Slavic pagan beliefs harbored towards the Christian clergy, even as the new faith gained a foothold in the lands of Kievan Rus'. This passage describes the arrival of Metropolitan John, a eunuch, and the subsequent reaction of the people, provides a glimpse into the complex interaction between pre-Christian Slavic beliefs about death, the afterlife, and the perception of those who were seen as different or otherworldly within the context of a Christianizing society.

Upon seeing Metropolitan John, the people's remark, "Behold, a dead person has come," can be interpreted through the lens of Slavic native faith, where the concept of death and the afterlife was often shrouded in mystery and superstition. In Slavic paganism, the line between the living and the dead was not always clear-cut. There were beliefs in spirits and revenants – beings thought to have returned from the dead. Such entities were often met with a mix of reverence, fear, and curiosity, as they were believed to possess knowledge or powers from the beyond.

Metropolitan John's status as a eunuch might have further contributed to this perception. In many ancient and pagan cultures, eunuchs were viewed as having a unique, often ambiguous, spiritual status due to their distinct physicality. They were sometimes associated with mystical or prophetic abilities, which could align with pagan beliefs in individuals who bridged the mortal and spiritual realms.

Moreover, the description of John as "not an erudite man, but poor in spirit and simple in conversation" might suggest a certain kind of spiritual wisdom valued in Slavic Native Faith. Unlike the Christian emphasis on theological learning and doctrinal understanding, in Slavic paganism, wisdom and spiritual insight could also be associated with humility, simplicity, and an innate connection to the natural and spiritual worlds.

The reaction to Metropolitan John and his subsequent death after a year, as narrated in the Chronicle, reflects a society where Christian and pagan beliefs coexisted and intertwined. The interpretation of John's presence and character traits through pagan beliefs about the afterlife and supernatural beings shows the persistence of these traditional beliefs among the populace.

Column. 208 - The Primary Chronicle

"Jan'ka brought Metropolitan John, a eunuch, with her; on seeing him everyone said: "Behold, a dead person has come". He lived for one year and then he died. He was not an erudite man, but poor in spirit and simple in conversation.".

SUPERNATURAL PHENOMENA & THE INFERNAL HUNT, C./214–215

The section talks of the mysterious, supernatural occurrences in Polotsk, where malevolent demonic presences terrorize the populace, interweaves with the ancient motif of the "infernal hunt," shedding light into the enduring power of folklore across Indo-European cultures. This passage, set against a backdrop of atmospheric anomalies and a significant drought, encapsulates a period where natural disasters and supernatural phenomena were deeply intertwined in the people's collective consciousness.

In Slavic Native Faith, the natural and supernatural worlds were closely linked, with spirits, demons, and deities playing an integral role in the people's lives. The events in Polotsk, described as demonic beings causing harm to those who ventured outside, resonate with these beliefs, portraying a world where supernatural entities wield tangible power over the physical realm. The fear instilled by these occurrences, compelling people to stay indoors, underscores the profound impact of such beliefs on daily life and societal norms.

The mention of the "infernal hunt," a folklore motif common to many Indo-European traditions, including Slavic, Germanic, and Celtic cultures, suggests a shared mythological heritage that transcends geographic and cultural boundaries. This spectral procession, often associated with wild hunts led by gods or legendary heroes across the sky or land, is imbued with various meanings, from harbingers of doom to conveyors of the souls of the dead. Its appearance in the Chronicle, linked to the sight of invisible riders and a significant circle in the sky, hints at a collective understanding of these phenomena as signs of otherworldly forces at play.

Furthermore, the connection between these supernatural events and subsequent natural disasters, like the drought and widespread fires, points to an interpretation of natural phenomena through a spiritual lens. In the Slavic pagan worldview, such events could be seen as manifestations of divine displeasure or warnings from the gods, requiring interpretation and propitiation.

The later reference to a dead person among the living, not causing death but perhaps signaling its presence in an unsettling manner, ties into ancient beliefs regarding the dead's influence on the living world. This notion suggests a permeable boundary between life and death, where the deceased could still affect the living, a concept prevalent in Slavic and broader

Indo-European pagan traditions.

This account does not merely recount a series of isolated incidents but weave together a complex narrative that reflects the Slavic native faith's depth and the cultural significance of folklore.

Column. 214-215 - The Primary Chronicle

> *"Something very strange occurred in Polotsk, a hallucination: there was a noise during the night: demons were running through the street like people. If anyone came out of their house to look, they were immediately and invisibly wounded by the demons and died of it, and they did not dare leave their houses. Then they began to appear during the day on horseback, and they themselves could not be seen, but only their horses' hooves were visible. And this is how they wounded the people of Polotsk and of the region. And this is why the people said: "The dead85 are slaying the people of Polotsk". This phenomenon began in Drjutsk. In the same period, there was a phenomenon in the sky, when a vast circle appeared in the middle of the sky. That year there was a drought, so the earth dried up and many forests and marshes caught fire. There were many phenomena (...).."*

SVAROG AND DAZHBOG: BRIDGING SLAVIC DEITIES C./278-279

These sections detail the reigns of Mestrom, Hermes, Hephaestus (identified with the Slavic god Svarog). His son (equated with Dazhbog), along with the introduction of laws and societal norms during Hephaestus/Svarog's time, provides a fascinating glimpse into how Slavic mythology and pre-Christian Slavic native faith interpreted and integrated stories from other cultures, notably Egyptian and Greek mythology. This passage, particularly with its focus on the year 1114 (6622) and the inclusion of glosses by the Slavic author, showcases the syncretism present in the Slavic adaptation of these myths and the identification of Greek deities with Slavic gods.

The identification of Hephaestus with Svarog, a deity associated with fire, and the son of Hephaestus with Dazhbog, a solar deity, reflects the Slavic effort to understand foreign myths within their own religious framework. Svarog's reign, characterized by the introduction of forging weapons and establishing laws around marriage and chastity, is depicted as a transformative period. This adaptation of Hephaestus's story to include Svarog suggests integrating the concept of civilization's progress—moving from primitive tools to forged weapons and from lawlessness to regulated social norms—into the Slavic mythological narrative.

The narrative underscores the cultural and religious flexibility of the Slavs in incorporating elements from other civilizations into their own beliefs, a testament to the interactions and exchanges between different cultures and religions. The passage also highlights the moral and societal values attributed to these deities, such as the emphasis on monogamy and the punishment for adultery, reflecting broader themes in Slavic native faith regarding order, justice, and societal norms.

Moreover, the mention of Dazhbog actions to uphold his father Svarog's laws further illustrates the continuation of these divine mandates and the importance of divine justice in maintaining societal purity and order. The execution of these laws by Dazhbog and the subsequent reverence he receives underscores the role of the sacred in guiding and protecting societal morals and values in Slavic Native Faith belief.

Column. 278-279 - The Primary Chronicle

"And after the flood and the division of the languages, the first to reign was Mestrom, of the line of Cam, after him Hermes, after him Hephaestus, whom the Egyptians call Svarog. During the reign of Hephaestus in Egypt, at the time of his reign, tongs fell from the sky and he began to forge weapons, as before they beat each other with sticks and stones. This Hephaestus established the law that women should marry a single man and behave in a chaste way, and he ordered that those who committed adultery should be punished. For this reason, he was also called the god Svarog, as before this women fornicated with whomsoever they wished and fornicated with cattle. If they gave birth to a child they gave it to whoever they wished: "Here is your child". And the person held a feast and accepted it. But Hephaestus eliminated this law and decreed that a man should have one wife and that a woman should marry a single man, and that if anyone were to violate (that law), they should be thrown into a fiery furnace; this is why he was called Svarog, and the Egyptians blessed him. And after him reigned his son, called Sun, who was known as

Daždbog, for seven thousand four hundred and seventy days, which make twenty and a half years. Because neither the Egyptians (nor) others knew how to count; some counted by the moon and others counted the years by days; the figure of 12 months was known later, from the time that men began to pay tax to the emperors. The emperor Sun, son of Svarog, who is Daždbog, was a strong man. Having heard from someone that a certain Egyptian woman, who was rich and respected, that someone wished to fornicate with her, he sought her to apprehend her so she did not break the law of her father Svarog. Taking with him some of his men, having discovered the moment at which the adultery would take place by night, he surprised her and did not find her husband with her but found her lying with another, with who she wanted. He seized her and tortured her and ordered her to be taken around the country for opprobrium and he beheaded her lover. And life was pure in all Egypt, and they began to praise him."

CONCLUSION

In our journey's final thoughts, we witnessed the stark display of a culture in transition, its ancient gods dragged through the mud and set aflame. Vladimir's decisive act of converting Rus to Christianity is not merely the end of an era but a new beginning painted in the somber tones of sacrifice and salvation. As the idols fall, so does the curtain on a pagan world, ushering in a baptism not just of faith but of fire and blood.

Yet, within the ashes of the old, the seeds of the future sprout, resilient and steadfast. The old gods may have been forgotten, yet they linger in whispered legends and the silent reverence of those who remember. Thus, the narrative of the Rus'—now Christian—continues its soul in defiance and devotion. The book closes on a note of solemn reflection: the journey of faith is both a path of destruction and a road to renewal, each step a testament to the enduring struggle between legacy and destiny. Beyond the last written page, the saga of the Slavs does not end but deepens. The spirit of the ancient faiths persists in villages and across vast fields beneath the very stones of the city streets. It is a quiet persistence, like the slow erosion of rock by wind—invisible, yet inevitable. The new faith roots itself in the rich soil of Rus', but it does so, intertwining with the tendrils of the old beliefs. Christianity adapts and absorbs, taking on hues of the native palette, a syncretism that is as much a compromise as it is a conquest.

As the voices of the old gods fade into the hinterlands of memory and myth, their stories are retold with a Christian gloss. Yet, these tales, like the characters within them, refuse to be fully tamed by the narratives imposed upon them. They rebel subtly, their pagan vitality bleeding through the veneers of saintly tales and churchly doctrines. This rebellion is not loud; it does not thunder across the steppes as did Perun's chariot. It is the whisper of the forest, the murmur of the river, the creak of the frost-laden branch—all speaking still of a world animated by forces older and wilder than any doctrine can fully tame.

In this way, the book is never fully closed. Each generation turns back the pages, finds new meaning in old words, and questions the certainties of the past. The tale of the Rus' becomes not a relic to be archived away in the dim light of a monastery library but a living story, continually rewritten in the hearts and minds of those who walk the land. The conclusion of this book is not an ending but an invitation—a call to look deeper, to remember, and perhaps, to begin again.

The Primary Chronicle is a foundation for studying Slavic paganism because it bridges the chasm between oral traditions and the written word. As the most comprehensive early account of Kievan Rus', it documents a transformative era. Through its narratives, we have seen the festivals, the gods like Perun and Veles, and the deeply rooted mythologies that shaped Slavic identity before the Christian overlay.

This text demonstrates how deeply ingrained pagan traditions refused to vanish quietly, instead morphing to fit new paradigms and continuing to influence the spiritual landscape of Eastern Europe well beyond the medieval period.

We stand here knowing that the quiet of twilight, where shadows blend with the fading light, the whispers of the past, and the rustle of old parchment seem to combine into a single breath of spirit. The Primary Chronicle, a venerable tome, sits heavily on the wooden table of history, its pages a palimpsest of ancient and adopted beliefs. As dusk deepens, it feels like the old Slavic gods cloaked now in half-forgotten tales stir beneath the lines of text, their stories pulsing through the Chronicle like the earth's heartbeat. The tales of pagan faith in this book does not merely recount history; it summons it, invoking the spirit of a people forever poised between the memory of what was and the mystery of what might yet be.

ABOUT THE AUTHORS

Perun Mountain is a cultural initiative and pen name by Philip and Paul, who are pioneers in preserving and promoting Slavic culture. This organization dedicates itself to translating Slavic manuscripts, enhancing cultural comprehension, and authoring works under the Perun Mountain alias to captivate a global readership.

Philip founded Perun Mountain, and is operated out of Northern New Hampshire, USA. As an adjunct college professor and professional lecturer, he infuses his academic pursuits with a genuine personal commitment to the Slavic traditions. His contributions transcend academic teaching as he delves into creating Slavic arts and literature, demonstrating his commitment to safeguarding Slavic cultural legacy.

Paul, hailing from Kyiv, Ukraine, plays a pivotal role in the team. Known for his exceptional translation abilities and linguistic prowess, Paul is essential in making Slavic texts accessible internationally.

Our Mission

Perun Mountain is devoted to celebrating and spreading Slavic art, music, and handicrafts while offering accurate and enriching insights into the Slavic Native Faith. This book represents the culmination of our endeavors to celebrate and propagate the wealth of Slavic spiritual and cultural heritage, making it an essential resource for those drawn to this rich tradition.

Slava!

www.PerunMountain.com

SLAVIC PAGAN ROOTS

Printed in Dunstable, United Kingdom